Cakes: Cheesecakes –

Step by Step Recipes of Decadent Cakes

MARIA SOBININA

BRILLIANTkitchenideas.com

Copyright © 2019 MARIA SOBININA
BRILLIANT kitchen ideas

All rights reserved.

ISBN: 9781981087648

DEDICATION

This book is dedicated to my beautiful family and friends, as well as to you, my reader. I am happy to share the amazing joy of baking with you.

MARIA XOXO

TABLE OF CONTENTS

Plain Vanilla Cheesecake *(Cookie Dough Crust)*   3

Plain Vanilla Cheesecake *(Graham Cookies Crust)*   9

Cheesecake with Figs and Walnuts   14

White Chocolate Raspberry Cheesecake   20

Chocolate Carrot Cheesecake   26

Chocolate Raspberry Cheesecake   33

Key Lime Cheesecake   40

Black Forest Cheesecake   46

Black Forest Merengue Cheesecake   53

Kahlua Cheesecake   62

Oreo Cookies Cheesecake   68

Wild Blueberries Cheesecake   74

Red Velvet Cheesecake   82

Nutella Cheesecake   89

Snickers Peanut Butter Cheesecake   96

Tropical Paradise Cheesecake   103

Plain Vanilla Cheesecake *(Cookie Dough Crust)*

INGREDIENTS:

FOR THE CAKE:

1 ½ cups **Flour**, all-purpose

1/2 cup **Butter**, unsalted, melted

1/2 cup **Sugar,** white, cane, granulated

1/2 cup **Sugar**, brown

1 **Egg**

2 tablespoons **Buttermilk** (or **Sour cream**)

1 teaspoon **Baking Powder**

3/4 teaspoon **Baking Soda**

1/4 teaspoon **Salt,** sea, fine

2 teaspoons **Vanilla**, extract, pure

Cooking spray for greasing the springform pan

FOR THE CHEESE:

24 Oz **Cream Cheese**

3 **Eggs**

1 cup **Sugar,** white, cane, granulated

3/4 cup **Sour Cream**

1 tablespoon **Flour,** all purpose

1/2 teaspoon **Vanilla**, extract, pure

FOR THE FROSTING:

6 Oz **Butter**, unsalted, softened

6 Oz **Farmer Cheese**

4 cups **Sugar**, white, cane, powdered

1 teaspoon **Vanilla**, extract, pure

EQUIPMENT:

One 9-inch springform baking pan, One larger ovenproof tray or pan to fit 9-inch springform pan, Aluminum foil, Stand or hand mixer fitted with the paddle attachment, Large mixing bowl, Spatula or cake scraper, Parchment paper, Cake decorating piping tips and bags (optional).

PREPARATION:

MAKE THE CAKE:

Step 1: Line the bottom of the 9-inch springform pan with parchment paper. Grease the paper and the sides of the pan with a cooking spray.

Step 2: In a large bowl, sift and combine flour, baking powder, baking soda, and salt. Set the flour mixture aside.

Step 3: Combine butter, sugar, brown sugar and eggs in a bowl of stand mixer fitted with the paddle attachment (you can use a bowl and a hand mixer).

Mix on low speed until everything is incorporated and batter achieves a smooth consistency. Add vegetable oil, buttermilk, sour cream, and vanilla extract. Continue mixing until all is incorporated.

Step 4: Separate flour mixture onto 3 or 4 parts and add it in 3 or 4 batches, using a spatula to fold in the mixture. Set aside.

MAKE THE CHEESE:

Step 1: In a bowl of a stand mixer beat cream cheese with the paddle attachment on low speed until it becomes smooth.

Step 2: Add sour cream, eggs, vanilla extract, and flour (little by little). Beat the mixture with the paddle attachment until it becomes smooth. Do not overbeat or the cake will crack.

ASSEMBLE THE CAKE:

Step 1: Pour cake batter into the greased springform pan. Pour cheese batter over the cake batter.

Step 2: Prepare the water-bath. Cover the bottom of springform pan with aluminum foil. Place it into a larger ovenproof tray. Pour one inch of boiling water into the larger tray. (Do not let water get into the cheesecake).

BAKE THE CAKE:

Step 1: Preheat the oven to 325F. Bake the cake for about one hour and ten minutes, or until the center is set and not very wobbly. At 30-35 minutes into baking, cover the springform pan with aluminum foil to prevent burning of the top of the cake.

Step 2: After one hour and ten minutes turn the oven off and leave the cheesecake inside the oven (with oven door closed) for another two hours.

Step 3: After two hours, set it aside to cool at room temperature. Cheesecake tastes best the next day. Once cheesecake is cooled to a room temperature leave it overnight in the fridge.

MAKE THE FROSTING:

Step 1: Combine butter and powdered sugar in a bowl of stand mixer fitted with the paddle attachment (you can use a bowl and a hand mixer).

Beat on medium speed for 2 to 3 minutes until it is fully incorporated and becomes fluffy and light in color.

Step 2: Spoon by spoon, add farmers cheese and beat on medium speed for 2 to 3 minutes until it is fully incorporated and becomes light and fluffy.

Add vanilla extract and beat for another 2-3 minutes.

If you decorate your cake, using cake decorating piping tips and bags, set aside and refrigerate 1/3 of the frosting for about an hour until it becomes firm.

This will be your cooled frosting. The rest of the frosting will be room temperature frosting.

Step 3: Spread the room temperature frosting over your cake. Level the edges and surface of the cake with a spatula or scraper. Sprinkle the top of the cake with shredded coconut.

Use cooled frosting to decorate the cake using piping tips and bags.

DECORATE THE CAKE:

If you are decorating your cake with cake decorating tools, once you are ready to decorate your cake, remove the cooled frosting from the fridge.

Place the cooled frosting into a piping bag and start piping borders and flowers. You can also add food coloring. *(We recommend using natural food coloring instead of artificial colors).*

Plain Vanilla Cheesecake will keep for up to five days in a fridge or one month in a freezer.

Plain Vanilla Cheesecake *(Graham Cookies Crust)*

INGREDIENTS:

FOR THE CAKE:

2 cups **Graham cookies,** Honey Maid brand

1 ½ cups **Butter**, unsalted, softened

1/2 cup **Sugar,** cane, granulated

Cooking spray for greasing the springform pan

FOR THE CHEESE:

32 Oz **Cream Cheese**

4 **Eggs**

1 ¼ cup **Sour cream**

1 cup **Sugar,** white, cane, granulated

3 tablespoon **Flour,** all purpose

1/2 teaspoon **Vanilla**, extract, pure

FOR THE FROSTING:

6 Oz **Butter**, unsalted, softened

6 Oz **Farmer Cheese,** or **Cream Cheese**

2 ½ cups **Sugar**, white, cane, powdered

1 teaspoon **Vanilla**, extract, pure

EQUIPMENT:

One 9-inch springform baking pan, One larger ovenproof tray or pan to fit 9-inch springform, Aluminum foil, Stand or hand mixer fitted with the paddle attachment, Large mixing bowl, Spatula or cake scraper, Parchment paper, Cake decorating piping tips and bags (optional).

PREPARATION:

MAKE THE CAKE:

Step 1: Preheat the oven to 350°F. Line the bottom of the 9-inch springform pan with parchment paper. Grease the paper and the sides of the pan with a cooking spray.

Step 2: Add graham cookies into a food processor and process into fine crumbs. Add melted butter and sugar. Process again until all is incorporated.

Step 3: Press the cookie mixture into the greased springform pan.

Step 4: Bake it for 10-15 minutes on 350°F. Set aside to cool. Reduce the oven's temperature to 325°F.

MAKE THE CHEESE:

Step 1: Add all cream cheese into a bowl of stand mixer (or use a large bowl and hand mixer with paddle attachment) equipped with the paddle attachment. Beat on low to medium until cream cheese softens and becomes smooth.

Step 2: Add sour cream, eggs, vanilla extract, sugar, and flour into the bowl with cream cheese. Beat the mixture with the paddle attachment until all is evenly incorporated and mixture becomes smooth. Do not overbeat, or the cake will crack.

ASSEMBLE THE CAKE:

Step 1: Pour cheese mixture over the graham cookies crust. Level with a spatula.

Step 2: Prepare the water-bath. Cover the bottom of springform pan with aluminum foil. Place it into a larger ovenproof tray. Pour one inch of boiling water into the larger tray. (Do not let water get into the cheesecake).

BAKE THE CAKE:

Step 1: Bake the cake at 325°F for about one hour and ten minutes or until the center of the cake is set and not very wobbly. At 30-35 minutes into baking, cover the springform with aluminum foil to prevent burning of the top of the cake.

Step 2: After one hour and ten minutes turn the oven off and leave the cheesecake inside the oven (with oven door closed) for two hours.

Step 3: After two hours, set it aside to cool at room temperature. Cheesecake tastes best the next day. Once the cheesecake is cooled to a room temperature leave it overnight in the fridge.

MAKE THE FROSTING:

Step 1: Combine butter and powdered sugar in a bowl of stand mixer fitted with the paddle attachment (you can use a bowl and a hand mixer).

Beat on medium speed for 2 to 3 minutes until it is fully incorporated and becomes fluffy and light in color.

Step 2: Spoon by spoon, add farmers cheese and beat on medium speed for 2 to 3 minutes until it is fully incorporated and becomes light and fluffy.

Add vanilla extract and beat for another 2-3 minutes.

If you decorate your cake, using cake decorating piping tips and bags, set aside and refrigerate 1/3 of the frosting for about an hour until it becomes firm.

This will be your cooled frosting. The rest of the frosting will be room temperature frosting. Cover top of cheesecake with frosting. Sprinkle with shredded coconut.

DECORATE THE CAKE:

If you are decorating your cake with cake decorating tools, once you are ready to decorate your cake, remove the cooled frosting from the fridge.

Place the cooled frosting into a piping bag and start piping borders and flowers. You can also add food coloring. *(We recommend using natural food coloring instead of artificial colors).*

Plain Vanilla Cheesecake will keep for up to five days in a fridge or one month in a freezer.

Cheesecake with Figs and Walnuts

INGREDIENTS:

FOR THE CAKE:

1 ½ cups **Flour**, all-purpose

1/2 cup **Butter**, unsalted, melted

1/2 cup **Sugar,** white, cane, granulated

1/2 cup **Sugar**, brown

1 **Egg**

2 tablespoons **Buttermilk** (or **Sour cream**)

1 teaspoon **Baking Powder**

3/4 teaspoon **Baking Soda**

1/4 teaspoon **Salt,** sea, fine

2 teaspoons **Vanilla**, extract, pure

Cooking spray for greasing the springform pan

FOR THE CHEESE:

24 Oz **Cream Cheese**

3 **Eggs**

1 cup **Sugar,** white, cane, granulated

3/4 cup **Sour Cream**

1 tablespoon **Flour,** all purpose

1/2 teaspoon **Vanilla**, extract, pure

1 cup **Figs,** dried

FOR THE FROSTING:

3 Oz **Butter**, unsalted, softened

3 Oz **Farmer Cheese**

2 cups **Sugar**, white, cane, powdered

½ teaspoon **Vanilla**, extract, pure

FOR THE DECORATIONS:

3 **Figs,** fresh

EQUIPMENT:

One 9-inch springform baking pan, One larger ovenproof tray or pan to fit 9-inch springform pan, Aluminum foil, Stand or hand mixer fitted with the paddle attachment, Large mixing bowl, Kitchen knife, Spatula or cake scraper, Parchment paper, Cake decorating piping tips and bags (optional).

PREPARATION:

MAKE THE CAKE:

Step 1: Line the bottom of the 9-inch springform pan with parchment paper. Grease the paper and the sides of the pan with a cooking spray.

Step 2: In a large bowl, sift and combine flour, baking powder, baking soda, and salt. Set the flour mixture aside.

Step 3: Combine butter, sugar, brown sugar and eggs in a bowl of stand mixer fitted with the paddle attachment (you can use a bowl and a hand mixer).

Mix on low speed until everything is incorporated and batter achieves a smooth consistency. Add vegetable oil, buttermilk, sour cream, and vanilla extract. Continue mixing until all is incorporated.

Step 4: Separate flour mixture onto 3 or 4 parts and add it in 3 or 4 batches, using a spatula to fold in the mixture. Set aside.

MAKE THE CHEESE:

Step 1: In a bowl of a stand mixer beat cream cheese with the paddle attachment on low speed until it becomes smooth.

Step 2: Add sour cream, eggs, vanilla extract, and flour (little by little). Beat the mixture with the paddle attachment until it becomes smooth. Do not overbeat or the cake will crack.

Step 3: Cut dried figs onto small (1/4 inch) pieces. Place them into a small bowl, cover with warm water and set aside for 15 minutes to soften. Drain water. Remove excess water with a paper towel.

Fold in figs into the cheese mixture. Mix with a spatula until all is evenly incorporated.

ASSEMBLE THE CAKE:

Step 1: Pour cake batter into the greased springform pan. Pour cheese batter over the cake batter.

Step 2: Prepare the water-bath. Cover the bottom of springform pan with aluminum foil.

Place it into a larger ovenproof tray. Pour one inch of boiling water into the larger tray. (Do not let water get into the cheesecake).

BAKE THE CAKE:

Step 1: Preheat the oven to 325F. Bake the cake for about one hour and ten minutes, or until the center is set and not very wobbly. At 30-35 minutes into baking, cover the springform pan with aluminum foil to prevent burning of the top of the cake.

Step 2: After one hour and ten minutes turn the oven off and leave the cheesecake inside the oven (with oven door closed) for another two hours.

Step 3: After two hours, set it aside to cool at room temperature. Cheesecake tastes best the next day. Once cheesecake is cooled to a room temperature leave it overnight in the fridge.

MAKE THE FROSTING:

Step 1: Combine butter and powdered sugar in a bowl of stand mixer fitted with the paddle attachment (you can use a bowl and a hand mixer).

Beat on medium speed for 2 to 3 minutes until it is fully incorporated and becomes fluffy and light in color.

Step 2: Spoon by spoon, add farmers cheese and beat on medium speed for 2 to 3 minutes until it is fully incorporated and becomes light and fluffy.

Add vanilla extract and beat for another 2-3 minutes.

Step 3: Spread the frosting over your cake. Level the edges and surface of the cake with a spatula or scraper.

DECORATE THE CAKE:

Cut fresh figs each into four parts. Chop walnuts. Place walnuts on top of the cake. Place fig pieces on top of walnuts.

Cheesecake with Figs and Walnuts will keep for up to five days in a fridge or one month in a freezer.

White Chocolate Raspberry Cheesecake

INGREDIENTS:

FOR THE CAKE:

2 cups **Oreo cookies,** without cream (remove)

1 ½ cups **Butter**, unsalted, softened

1/2 cup **Sugar,** white, cane, granulated

Cooking spray for greasing the springform pan

FOR THE SYRUP:

12 Oz **Raspberries**, frozen

2 cups **Sugar,** white, cane, granulated

6 tablespoons **Water**

1 tablespoon **Cornstarch**, organic

1/2 tablespoon **Vanilla,** pure, extract

FOR THE CHEESE:

32 Oz **Cream Cheese**

4 **Eggs**

1 ¼ cup **Sour Cream**

1 cup **Sugar,** white, cane, granulated

1 tablespoon **Flour,** all purpose

1/2 tablespoon **Vanilla,** pure, extract

FOR THE FROSTING:

6 Oz **Farmer Cheese**

6 Oz **Butter**, unsalted, softened

2 ½ cups **Sugar**, white, cane, powdered

1/2 tablespoon **Vanilla,** extract, pure

FOR THE DECORATIONS:

1 cup **Chocolate**, white, shaved

8 Oz **Raspberries**, fresh

EQUIPMENT:

One 9-inch springform baking pan, One larger ovenproof tray or pan to fit 9-inch springform, Aluminum foil, Small saucepan, Stand or hand mixer fitted with the paddle attachment, Large mixing bowl, Spatula or cake scraper, Cake decorating piping tips and bags (optional).

PREPARATION:

Step 1: Preheat the oven to 350°F. Line the bottom of the 9-inch springform pan with parchment paper. Grease the paper and the sides of the pan with a cooking spray.

Step 2: In a food processor, add graham cookies and process into fine crumbs. Add melted butter and sugar. Process again until all is incorporated.

Step 3: Press the cookie mix into a greased springform pan.

Step 4: Bake it for 10-15 minutes on 350°F. Set aside to cool. Reduce the oven's temperature to 325°F.

MAKE THE SYRUP:

In a small saucepan combine raspberries, sugar, and water. Let the mixture boil over medium heat, constantly stirring it. Add cornstarch and vanilla.

Once the mixture thickens, turn off the heat and set the syrup aside to cool.

MAKE THE CHEESE:

Step 1: Add all cream cheese into a bowl of stand mixer (or use a large bowl and hand mixer with paddle attachment) equipped with the paddle attachment. Beat on low to medium until cream cheese softens and becomes smooth.

Step 2: Add sour cream, eggs, vanilla extract, sugar, and flour into the bowl with cream cheese. Beat the mixture with the paddle attachment until all is evenly incorporated and mixture becomes smooth. Do not overbeat, or the cake will crack.

Step 3: Fold in raspberry syrup, gently mixing with a spatula. Do not over mix. Leave small chunks of the raspberries cluster together.

ASSEMBLE THE CAKE:

Step 1: Pour cake batter into the greased springform pan. Pour raspberry cheese over the cake batter.

Step 2: Prepare the water-bath. Cover the bottom of springform pan with aluminum foil. Place it into a larger ovenproof tray. Pour one inch of boiling water into the larger tray. (Do not let water get into the cheesecake).

BAKE THE CAKE:

Step 1: Bake the cake at 325°F for about one hour and ten minutes or until the center of the cake is set and not very wobbly. At 30-35 minutes into baking, cover the springform with aluminum foil to prevent burning of the top of the cake.

Step 2: After one hour and ten minutes turn the oven off and leave the cheesecake inside the oven (with oven door closed) for two hours.

Step 3: After two hours, set it aside to cool at room temperature. Cheesecake tastes best the next day. Once the cheesecake is cooled to a room temperature leave it overnight in the fridge.

MAKE THE FROSTING:

Step 1: Combine butter and powdered sugar in a bowl of stand mixer fitted with the paddle attachment (you can use a bowl and a hand mixer).

Beat on medium speed for 2 to 3 minutes until it is fully incorporated and becomes fluffy and light in color.

Step 2: Spoon by spoon, add farmers cheese and beat on medium speed for 2 to 3 minutes until it is fully incorporated and becomes light and fluffy.

Add vanilla extract and beat for another 2-3 minutes.

If you decorate your cake, using cake decorating piping tips and bags, set aside and refrigerate 1/3 of the frosting for about an hour until it becomes firm.

This will be your cooled frosting. The rest of the frosting will be room temperature frosting. Cover top of cheesecake with frosting. Sprinkle with shredded coconut. Decorate with fresh raspberries.

DECORATE THE CAKE:

If you are decorating your cake with cake decorating tools, once you are ready to decorate your cake, remove the cooled frosting from the fridge.

Place the cooled frosting into a piping bag and start piping borders and flowers. You can also add food coloring. *(We recommend using natural food coloring instead of artificial colors).*

White Chocolate Raspberry Cheesecake will keep for up to five days in a fridge or one month in a freezer.

Chocolate Carrot Cheesecake

INGREDIENTS:

FOR THE CAKE:

1 ½ cups **Flour**, all-purpose

3 **Eggs**

1 cup **Sugar,** cane, granulated

1/2 cup **Sugar**, brown

1 cup **Cocoa powder**, Dutch, unsweetened

1/2 cup **Carrots**, raw, peeled

1/2 cup **Dates,** dried, pitted

1/2 cup **Applesauce,** unsweetened

1/2 cup **Buttermilk**

1 teaspoon **Baking Powder**

3/4 teaspoon **Baking Soda**

3/4 teaspoon **Salt,** sea, fine

1 cup **Olive Oil,** virgin, cold pressed

1 teaspoon **Cinnamon**, ground

Cooking spray for greasing springform pan

FOR THE CHEESE:

24 Oz **Cream Cheese**

3 **Eggs**

1 cup **Sugar,** cane, granulated

1 cup **Sour Cream**

1/4 cup **Buttermilk**

1 tablespoon **Flour,** all purpose

FOR THE FROSTING:

6 Oz **Farmer Cheese**

6 Oz **Butter**, unsalted, softened

2 ½ cups **Sugar**, cane, powdered

1/2 tablespoon **Vanilla,** pure, extract

FOR THE DECORATIONS:

1 cup **Coconut**, unsweetened, shredded

EQUIPMENT:

One 9-inch springform baking pan, One larger ovenproof tray or pan to fit 9-inch springform, Aluminum foil, Stand or hand mixer fitted with the paddle attachment, Large mixing bowls, Food processor or hand grater, Spatula or cake scraper, Parchment paper, Cake decorating piping tips and bags (optional).

PREPARATION:

MAKE THE CAKE:

Step 1: Place dates into a small bowl, cover with water and set aside for one hour to soften.

Step 2: Line the bottom of the 9-inch springform pan with parchment paper. Grease the paper and the sides of the pan with a cooking spray.

Step 3: Grate the carrots in a food processor (or with a hand grater).

Step 4: In a large bowl, combine flour, cocoa powder, baking powder, baking soda, and salt.

Step 5: Combine sugar and eggs in a bowl of stand mixer fitted with the paddle attachment (you can use a bowl and a hand mixer).
Mix on low speed until everything is well incorporated and achieves a smooth consistency.

Add vegetable oil, buttermilk, vanilla, and applesauce. Continue mixing until all is well incorporated.

Step 6: Separate flour mixture onto 3 or 4 parts and add it in 3 or 4 batches, using a spatula to fold the mixture together until all is incorporated. Set aside. Fold in carrots mixing with a spatula. Set aside.

MAKE THE CHEESE:

Step 1: Add all cream cheese into a bowl of stand mixer (or use a large bowl and hand mixer with paddle attachment) equipped with the paddle attachment. Beat on low to medium until cream cheese softens and becomes smooth.

Step 2: Add buttermilk, sour cream, sugar, eggs, and flour (little by little). Beat the mixture with the paddle attachment until it becomes smooth. Do not overbeat or the cake will crack.

ASSEMBLE THE CAKE:

Step 1: Pour 1/3 of cake batter into a greased springform pan. Pour 1/3 of cheese batter over the cake batter.

Step 2: Repeat until you use all cake and cheese batters.
You can swirl it with a wooden skewer to create a "marbled" effect.

Step 3: Prepare the water-bath. Cover the bottom of springform pan with aluminum foil. Place it into a larger ovenproof tray. Pour one inch of boiling water into the larger tray. (Do not let water get into the cheesecake).

BAKE THE CAKE:

Step 1: Preheat the oven to 325°F.

Bake the cake for about one hour and ten minutes, or until the center is set and not very wobbly. At 30-35 minutes into baking, cover the springform with aluminum foil to prevent burning of the top of the cake.

Step 2: After one hour and ten minutes turn the oven off and leave the cheesecake inside the oven (with oven door closed) for another two hours.

Step 3: After two hours, set it aside to cool at room temperature. Cheesecake tastes best the next day. Once the cheesecake is cooled to a room temperature leave it overnight in the fridge.

MAKE THE FROSTING:

Step 1: Combine butter and powdered sugar in a bowl of stand mixer fitted with the paddle attachment (you can use a bowl and a hand mixer).

Beat on medium speed for 2 to 3 minutes until it is fully incorporated and becomes fluffy and light in color.

Step 2: Spoon by spoon, add farmers cheese and beat on medium speed for 2 to 3 minutes until it is fully incorporated and becomes light and fluffy.

Add vanilla extract and beat for another 2-3 minutes.

If you decorate your cake, using cake decorating piping tips and bags, set aside and refrigerate 1/3 of the frosting for about an hour until it becomes firm.

This will be your cooled frosting. The rest of the frosting will be room temperature frosting.

Step 3: Spread the room temperature frosting over your cake. Level the edges and surface of the cake with a spatula or scraper.

Use cooled frosting to decorate the cake using piping tips and bags.

DECORATE THE CAKE:

If you are decorating your cake with cake decorating tools, once you are ready to decorate your cake, remove the cooled frosting from the fridge.

Place the cooled frosting into a piping bag and start piping borders and flowers. You can also add food coloring. *(We recommend using natural food coloring instead of artificial colors).*

Chocolate Carrot Cheesecake will keep for up to five days in a fridge or one month in a freezer.

Chocolate Raspberry Cheesecake

INGREDIENTS:

FOR THE CAKE:

1 ½ cups **Flour**, all-purpose

1/2 cup **Butter**, unsalted, melted

1/2 cup **Sugar,** cane, granulated

1/2 cup **Sugar**, brown

1/2 cup **Cocoa powder**, Dutch, unsweetened

1 **Egg**

2 tablespoons **Buttermilk** (or **Sour Cream**)

1 teaspoon **Baking Powder**

3/4 teaspoon **Baking Soda**

1/4 teaspoon **Salt,** fine, sea

2 teaspoons **Vanilla**, extract, pure

Cooking spray for greasing the springform pan

FOR THE SYRUP:

1/2 cup **Raspberry Preserve**, seedless

6 tablespoons **Water**

1 tablespoon **Cornstarch**, organic

1/2 tablespoon **Vanilla,** pure, extract

FOR THE CHEESE:

24 Oz **Cream Cheese**

3 **Eggs**

1 cup **Sugar,** cane, granulated

1/2 cup **Cocoa powder**, Dutch, unsweetened

1 cup **Sour Cream**

1 tablespoon **Flour,** all purpose

1/2 teaspoon **Vanilla**, extract, pure

FOR THE FROSTING:

6 Oz **Farmer Cheese**

6 Oz **Butter**, unsalted, softened

2 ½ cups **Sugar**, cane, powdered

1/2 tablespoon **Vanilla,** pure, extract

FOR THE DECORATIONS:

1 cup **Raspberries**, fresh

EQUIPMENT:

One 9-inch springform baking pan, One larger ovenproof tray or pan to fit 9-inch springform, Aluminum foil, Small saucepan, Stand or hand mixer fitted with the paddle attachment, Large mixing bowls, Food processor or hand grater, Spatula or cake scraper, Parchment paper, Cake decorating piping tips and bags (optional).

PREPARATION:

MAKE THE CAKE:

Step 1: Line the bottom of the 9-inch springform pan with parchment paper. Grease the paper and the sides of the pan with a cooking spray.

Step 2: In a large bowl, sift and combine flour, baking powder, baking soda, and salt. Set the flour mixture aside.

Step 3: Combine butter, sugar, brown sugar and eggs in a bowl of stand mixer fitted with the paddle attachment (you can use a bowl and a hand mixer).

Mix on low speed until everything is incorporated and batter achieves a smooth consistency. Add vegetable oil, buttermilk, and vanilla extract. Continue mixing until all is incorporated.

Step 4: Separate flour mixture onto 3 or 4 parts and add it in 3 or 4 batches, using a spatula to fold the mixture together until all is incorporated. Set aside.

MAKE THE SYRUP:

In a small saucepan combine raspberries, sugar, and water. Let the mixture boil over medium heat, constantly stirring it. Add cornstarch and vanilla.

Once the mixture thickens, turn off the heat and set the syrup aside to cool.

MAKE THE CHEESE:

Step 1: Add all cream cheese into a bowl of stand mixer (or use a large bowl and hand mixer with paddle attachment) equipped with the paddle attachment. Beat on low to medium until cream cheese softens and becomes smooth.

Step 2: Add sugar, eggs, sour cream, cocoa powder, vanilla extract, and flour (little by little). Beat the mixture with the paddle attachment until it becomes smooth. Do not overbeat or the cake will crack.

Step 3: Fold in raspberry syrup, gently mixing with a spatula. Do not over mix. Leave small chunks of the raspberries cluster together.

ASSEMBLE THE CAKE:

Step 1: Pour cake batter into the greased springform pan. Pour raspberry cheese over the cake batter.

Step 2: Prepare the water-bath. Cover the bottom of springform pan with aluminum foil. Place it into a larger ovenproof tray. Pour one inch of boiling water into the larger tray. (Do not let water get into the cheesecake).

BAKE THE CAKE:

Step 1: Preheat the oven to 325F.

Bake the cake for about one hour and ten minutes, or until the center is set and not very wobbly. At 30-35 minutes into baking, cover the springform with aluminum foil to prevent burning of the top of the cake.

Step 2: After one hour and ten minutes turn the oven off and leave the cheesecake inside the oven (with oven door closed) for another two hours.

Step 3: After two hours, set it aside to cool at room temperature. Cheesecake tastes best the next day. Once the cheesecake is cooled to a room temperature leave it overnight in the fridge.

MAKE THE FROSTING:

Step 1: Combine butter and powdered sugar in a bowl of stand mixer fitted with the paddle attachment (you can use a bowl and a hand mixer).

Beat on medium speed for 2 to 3 minutes until it is fully incorporated and becomes fluffy and light in color.

Step 2: Spoon by spoon, add farmers cheese and beat on medium speed for 2 to 3 minutes until it is fully incorporated and becomes light and fluffy.

Add vanilla extract and beat for another 2-3 minutes.

If you decorate your cake, using cake decorating piping tips and bags, set aside and refrigerate 1/3 of the frosting for about an hour until it becomes firm.

This will be your cooled frosting. The rest of the frosting will be room temperature frosting.

Step 3: Spread the room temperature frosting over your cake. Level the edges and surface of the cake with a spatula or scraper. Decorate with fresh raspberries.

Use cooled frosting to decorate the cake using piping tips and bags.

DECORATE THE CAKE:

If you are decorating your cake with cake decorating tools, once you are ready to decorate your cake, remove the cooled frosting from the fridge.

Place the cooled frosting into a piping bag and start piping borders and flowers. You can also add food coloring. *(We recommend using natural food coloring instead of artificial colors).*

Chocolate Raspberries Cheesecake will keep for up to five days in a fridge or one month in a freezer.

Key Lime Cheesecake

INGREDIENTS:

FOR THE CAKE CRUST:

2 cups **Graham cookies,** Honey Maid brand

1 ½ cups **Butter**, unsalted, softened

1/2 cup **Sugar,** cane, powdered

Cooking spray for greasing the springform pan

FOR THE CHEESE:

32 Oz **Cream Cheese**

3 **Eggs**

1 cup **Sugar,** granulated

1 ¼ cup **Sour Cream**

3/4 cup **Key Lime** juice

1 tablespoon **Flour,** all purpose

1/2 teaspoon **Vanilla**, extract, pure

FOR THE FROSTING:

6 Oz **Butter**, unsalted, softened

6 Oz **Farmer Cheese**

2 ½ cups **Sugar**, cane, powdered

1/4 cup **Key Lime** juice

1 teaspoon **Vanilla**, extract, pure

EQUIPMENT:

One 9-inch springform baking pan, One larger ovenproof tray or pan to fit 9-inch springform, Aluminum foil, Stand or hand mixer fitted with the paddle attachment, Large mixing bowl, Spatula or cake scraper, Parchment paper, Cake decorating piping tips and bags (optional).

PREPARATION:

MAKE THE CAKE CRUST:

Step 1: Preheat the oven to 350°F. Line the bottom of the 9-inch springform pan with parchment paper. Grease the paper and the sides of the pan with a cooking spray.

Step 2: In a food processor, add graham cookies and process into fine crumbs. Add melted butter and sugar. Process again until all is incorporated.

Step 3: Press the cookie mix into a greased springform pan.

Step 4: Bake it for 10-15 minutes on 350°F. Set aside to cool. Reduce the oven's temperature to 325°F.

MAKE THE CHEESE:

Step 1: Add all cream cheese into a bowl of stand mixer (or use a large bowl and hand mixer with paddle attachment) equipped with the paddle attachment. Beat on low to medium until cream cheese softens and becomes smooth.

Step 2: Add buttermilk, sour cream, sugar, eggs, lime juice, vanilla extract, and flour. Beat the mixture with the paddle attachment until all is evenly incorporated and mixture becomes smooth. Do not overbeat, or the cake will crack.

ASSEMBLE THE CAKE:

Step 1: Pour lime cheese batter over the graham cookies crust.

Step 2: Prepare the water-bath. Cover the bottom of springform pan with aluminum foil. Place it into a larger ovenproof tray. Pour one inch of boiling water into the larger tray. (Do not let water get into the cheesecake).

BAKE THE CAKE:

Step 1: Bake the cake at 325°F for about one hour and ten minutes or until the center of the cake is set and not very wobbly. At 30-35 minutes into baking, cover the springform with aluminum foil to prevent burning of the top of the cake.

Step 2: After one hour and ten minutes turn the oven off and leave the cheesecake inside the oven (with oven door closed) for two hours.

Step 3: After two hours, set it aside to cool at room temperature. Cheesecake tastes best the next day. Once the cheesecake is cooled to a room temperature leave it overnight in the fridge.

MAKE THE FROSTING:

Step 1: Combine butter and powdered sugar in a bowl of stand mixer fitted with the paddle attachment (you can use a bowl and a hand mixer).

Beat on medium speed for 2 to 3 minutes until it is fully incorporated and becomes fluffy and light in color.

Step 2: Spoon by spoon, add farmers cheese and beat on medium speed for 2 to 3 minutes until it is fully incorporated and becomes light and fluffy.

Add vanilla extract, key lime juice and beat for another 2-3 minutes.

If you decorate your cake, using cake decorating piping tips and bags, set aside and refrigerate 1/3 of the frosting for about an hour until it becomes firm.

This will be your cooled frosting. The rest of the frosting will be room temperature frosting. Cover top of cheesecake with frosting.

DECORATE THE CAKE:

If you are decorating your cake with cake decorating tools, once you are ready to decorate your cake, remove the cooled frosting from the fridge.

Place the cooled frosting into a piping bag and start piping borders and flowers. You can also add food coloring. *(We recommend using natural food coloring instead of artificial colors).*

Key Lime Cheesecake will keep for up to five days in a fridge or one month in a freezer.

Black Forest Cheesecake

INGREDIENTS:

FOR THE CAKE:

1 ½ cups **Flour**, all-purpose

1 **Egg**

1/2 cup **Butter**, unsalted, melted

1/2 cup **Sugar,** cane, granulated

1/2 cup **Sugar**, brown

1/2 cup **Cocoa Powder**, Dutch, unsweetened

2 tablespoons **Buttermilk (or Sour cream)**

1 teaspoon **Baking Powder**

3/4 teaspoon **Baking Soda**

1/4 teaspoon **Salt,** fine, sea

2 teaspoons **Vanilla**, extract, pure

Cooking spray for greasing the springform pan

FOR THE SYRUP:

12 Oz **Cherries**, frozen

1/2 cup **Sugar**, brown

6 tablespoons **Water**

1 tablespoon **Cornstarch**, organic

1/2 tablespoon **Vanilla,** pure, extract

FOR THE CHERRIES LAYER:

12 Oz **Cherries**, frozen, thawed

FOR THE CHEESE:

24 Oz **Cream Cheese**

3 **Eggs**

1 cup **Sugar,** cane, granulated

1 cup **Sour Cream**

1 tablespoon **Flour,** all purpose

1/2 teaspoon **Vanilla**, extract, pure

FOR THE FROSTING:

6 Oz **Farmer Cheese**

6 Oz **Butter**, unsalted, softened

2 ½ cups **Sugar**, powdered

1/2 tablespoon **Vanilla,** pure, extract

FOR THE DECORATIONS:

1 cup **Chocolate,** dark, shaved

25 **Cherries**, fresh, pitted

EQUIPMENT:

One 9-inch springform baking pan, One larger ovenproof tray or pan to fit 9-inch springform; aluminum foil, Small saucepan, Stand or hand mixer fitted with the paddle attachment, Large mixing bowl, Food processor or hand grater, Spatula or cake scraper, Parchment paper, Cake decorating piping tips and bags (optional).

PREPARATION:

MAKE THE CAKE:

Step 1: Line the bottom of the 9-inch springform pan with parchment paper.

Grease the paper and the sides of the pan with a cooking spray.

Step 2: In a large bowl, sift and combine flour, baking powder, baking soda, and salt. Set the flour mixture aside.

Step 3: Combine butter, sugar, brown sugar and eggs in a bowl of stand mixer fitted with the paddle attachment (you can use a bowl and a hand mixer).

Mix on low speed until everything is incorporated and batter achieves a smooth consistency. Add vegetable oil, buttermilk, and vanilla extract. Continue mixing until all is incorporated.

Step 4: Separate flour mixture onto 3 or 4 parts and add it in 3 or 4 batches, using a spatula to fold the mixture together until all is incorporated. Set aside.

MAKE THE SYRUP:

In a small saucepan combine frozen cherries, sugar, and water. Let the mixture boil over medium heat, constantly stirring it. Add cornstarch and vanilla.

Once the mixture thickens, turn off the heat and set the syrup aside to cool.

MAKE THE CHEESE:

Step 1: Add all cream cheese into a bowl of stand mixer (or use a large bowl and hand mixer with paddle attachment) equipped with the paddle attachment. Beat on low to medium until cream cheese softens and becomes smooth.

Step 2: Add sour cream, sugar, eggs, vanilla extract, and flour (little by little). Beat the mixture with the paddle attachment until it becomes smooth. Do not overbeat or the cake will crack.

Fold in cherry syrup and mix with a spatula until all is evenly mixed. Do not overmix. Let the cherry syrup stay in small chunks.

ASSEMBLE THE CAKE:

Step 1: Pour cake batter into the greased springform pan. Place thawed cherries onto the cake batter. Distribute evenly. Pour cherry cheese over thawed cherries layer.

Step 2: Prepare the water-bath. Cover the bottom of springform pan with aluminum foil.

Place it into a larger ovenproof tray. Pour one inch of boiling water into the larger tray. (Do not let water get into the cheesecake).

BAKE THE CAKE:

Preheat the oven to 325F.

Step 1: Bake the cake for about one hour and ten minutes, or until the center is set and not very wobbly. At 30-35 minutes into baking, cover the springform with aluminum foil to prevent burning of the top of the cake.

Step 2: After one hour and ten minutes turn the oven off and leave the cheesecake inside the oven (with oven door closed) for another two hours.

Step 3: After two hours, set it aside to cool at room temperature. Cheesecake tastes best the next day. Once the cheesecake is cooled to a room temperature leave it overnight in the fridge.

MAKE THE FROSTING:

Step 1: Combine butter and powdered sugar in a bowl of stand mixer fitted with the paddle attachment (you can use a bowl and a hand mixer).

Beat on medium speed for 2 to 3 minutes until it is fully incorporated and becomes fluffy and light in color.

Step 2: Spoon by spoon, add farmers cheese and beat on medium speed for 2 to 3 minutes until it is fully incorporated and becomes light and fluffy.

Add vanilla extract and beat for another 2-3 minutes.

If you decorate your cake, using cake decorating piping tips and bags, set aside and refrigerate 1/3 of the frosting for about an hour until it becomes firm.

This will be your cooled frosting. The rest of the frosting will be room temperature frosting.

DECORATE THE CAKE:

If you are decorating your cake with cake decorating tools, once you are ready to decorate your cake, remove the cooled frosting from the fridge.

Place the cooled frosting into a piping bag and start piping borders and flowers. You can also add food coloring. *(We recommend using natural food coloring instead of artificial colors).*

Black Forest Cheesecake will keep for up to five days in a fridge or one month in a freezer.

Black Forest Merengue Cheesecake

INGREDIENTS:

FOR THE CAKE:

1 ½ cups **Flour**, all-purpose

1/2 cup **Butter**, unsalted, melted

1/2 cup **Sugar,** granulated

1/2 cup **Sugar**, brown

1/2 cup **Cocoa powder**, Dutch, unsweetened

1 **Egg**

2 tablespoons **Buttermilk** (or **Sour cream**)

1 teaspoon **Baking Powder**

3/4 teaspoon **Baking Soda**

1/4 teaspoon **Salt**

2 teaspoons **Vanilla**, pure, extract

Cooking spray for greasing the springform pan

FOR THE SYRUP:

12 Oz **Cherries**, frozen

1/2 cup **Sugar**, brown

6 tablespoons **Water**

1 tablespoon **Cornstarch**, organic

1/2 tablespoon **Vanilla,** pure, extract

FOR THE MERINGUE:

4 **Egg,** whites, room temperature

1 cup **Sugar,** cane, powdered

1/3 teaspoon **Cream of Tartar**

1 teaspoon **Vanilla**, pure, extract

FOR THE CHERRIES MERINGUE:

12 Oz **Cherries**, frozen, thawed
Crumbled Meringues

FOR THE CHEESE:

24 Oz **Cream Cheese**

3 **Eggs**

1 cup **Sugar,** cane, granulated

1 cup **Sour Cream**

1 tablespoon **Flour,** all purpose

1/2 teaspoon **Vanilla**, extract, pure

FOR THE FROSTING:

6 Oz **Farmer Cheese**

6 Oz **Butter**, unsalted, softened

2 ½ cups **Sugar**, cane, powdered

1/2 tablespoon **Vanilla,** pure, extract

FOR THE DECORATIONS:

1 cup **Chocolate,** dark, shaved

25 **Cherries**, fresh, pitted

EQUIPMENT:

One 9-inch springform baking pan, One larger ovenproof tray or pan to fit 9-inch springform, Aluminum foil,

Small saucepan, Stand or hand mixer fitted with the paddle attachment, Large mixing bowl, Food processor or hand grater, Spatula or cake scraper, Parchment paper, Cake decorating piping tips and bags (optional).

PREPARATION:

MAKE THE CAKE:

Step 1: Line the bottom of the 9-inch springform pan with parchment paper. Grease the paper and the sides of the pan with a cooking spray.

Step 2: In a large bowl sift and combine flour, cocoa powder, baking powder, baking soda, and salt. Set the flour mixture aside.

Step 3: Combine butter, sugar, brown sugar and eggs in a bowl of stand mixer fitted with the paddle attachment (you can use a bowl and a hand mixer).

Mix on low speed until everything is incorporated and batter achieves a smooth consistency. Add vegetable oil, buttermilk, and vanilla extract. Continue mixing until all is incorporated.

Step 4: Separate flour mixture onto 3 or 4 parts and add it in 3 or 4 batches, using a spatula to fold the mixture together until all is incorporated. Set aside.

MAKE THE MERINGUE:

Preheat the oven to 250°F.

Step 1: Combine egg whites, cream of tartar, vanilla in a bowl of stand mixer fitted with the paddle attachment (you can use a bowl and a hand mixer). Beat on medium speed until foamy.

One spoon at a time, add sugar and beat until sugar dissolves, then add more sugar. Repeat. Continue beating for 7 to 10 minutes until still glossy peaks start forming.

Step 2: Take your pastry bag and set a decorating tip with a small hole. Alternatively, you can cut a small hole in the pastry piping bag.

Step 3: Transfer meringue to the piping bag. Pipe 1 ½ – 2-inch diameter cookies onto a large baking tray lined with parchment paper. Space them 2 inches apart.

On a small baking tray lined up with greased parchment paper, pipe smaller cookies (1/2 inches) for cake decorations. Space them 1 inch apart.

Step 4: Bake meringues on large tray 40-45 minutes or until firm to the touch. Twenty minutes into baking put small meringues into the oven.

Bake for another 25 minutes or until firm to touch. Turn off oven and leave meringues in oven for about 1 hour.

Step 5: Remove meringues from the oven, separate from the parchment paper. Set aside small meringues for cake decorations.

Turn large meringues into crumbs (approximately 1/4 inch. You can have a mix of larger and smaller crumbs.) Set aside.

MAKE THE SYRUP:

In a small saucepan combine frozen cherries, sugar, and water. Let the mixture boil over medium heat, constantly stirring it. Add cornstarch and vanilla.

Once the mixture thickens, turn off the heat and set the syrup aside to cool.

MAKE THE CHEESE:

Step 1: Add all cream cheese into a bowl of stand mixer (or use a large bowl and hand mixer with paddle attachment) equipped with the paddle attachment. Beat on low to medium until cream cheese softens and becomes smooth.

Step 2: Add sour cream, buttermilk, eggs, vanilla extract, and flour (little by little). Beat the mixture with the paddle attachment until it becomes smooth. Do not overbeat or the cake will crack.

Fold in cherry syrup. Mix with a spatula. Do not overmix.

ASSEMBLE THE CAKE:

Step 1: Pour cake batter into the greased springform pan. Place thawed cherries onto the cake butter. Distribute evenly.

Place crushed meringues on top of thawed cherries. Distribute evenly. Pour cherry cheese over the thawed cherries layer.

Step 2: Prepare the water-bath. Cover the bottom of springform pan with aluminum foil. Place it into a larger ovenproof tray. Pour one inch of boiling water into the larger tray. (Do not let water get into the cheesecake).

BAKE THE CAKE:

Step 1: Preheat the oven to 325F. Bake the cake for about one hour and ten minutes, or until the center is set and not very wobbly. At 30-35 minutes into baking, cover the springform with aluminum foil to prevent burning of the top of the cake.

Step 2: After one hour and ten minutes turn the oven off and leave the cheesecake inside the oven (with oven door closed) for another two hours.

Step 3: After two hours, set it aside to cool at room temperature. Cheesecake tastes best the next day. Once the cheesecake is cooled to a room temperature leave it overnight in the fridge.

MAKE THE FROSTING:

Step 1: Combine butter and powdered sugar in a bowl of stand mixer fitted with the paddle attachment (you can use a bowl and a hand mixer).

Beat on medium speed for 2 to 3 minutes until it is fully incorporated and becomes fluffy and light in color.

Step 2: Spoon by spoon, add farmers cheese and beat on medium speed for 2 to 3 minutes until it is fully incorporated and becomes light and fluffy.

Add vanilla extract and beat for another 2-3 minutes.

If you decorate your cake, using cake decorating piping tips and bags, set aside and refrigerate 1/3 of the frosting for about an hour until it becomes firm.

This will be your cooled frosting. The rest of the frosting will be room temperature frosting.

Step 3: Spread the room temperature frosting over your cake. Level the edges and surface of the cake with a spatula or scraper.

Use cooled frosting to decorate the cake using piping tips and bags.

DECORATE THE CAKE:

If you are decorating your cake with cake decorating tools, once you are ready to decorate your cake, remove the cooled frosting from the fridge.

Place the cooled frosting into a piping bag and start piping borders and flowers. You can also add food coloring. *(We recommend using natural food coloring instead of artificial colors).*

Black Forest Meringue Cheesecake will keep for up to five days in a fridge or one month in a freezer.

Kahlua Cheesecake

INGREDIENTS:

FOR THE CAKE:

2 cups **Graham cookies,** Honey Maid brand

1 ½ cups **Butter**, unsalted, softened

1/2 cup **Sugar,** cane, granulated

Cooking spray for greasing the springform pan

FOR THE CHEESE:

32 Oz **Cream Cheese**

4 **Eggs**

1 ¼ cup **Sour Cream**

1 cup **Sugar,** cane, granulated

1/2 cup **Kahlua**, liqueur

1 cup **Chocolate Chips,** dark

3 tablespoon **Flour,** all purpose

1/2 teaspoon **Vanilla**, extract, pure

FOR THE FROSTING:

6 Oz **Butter**, unsalted, softened

6 Oz **Farmer Cheese**

2 ½ cups **Sugar**, powdered

1/4 cup **Kahlua**, liqueur

1 teaspoon **Vanilla**, extract, pure

EQUIPMENT:

One 9-inch springform baking pan, One larger ovenproof tray or pan to fit 9-inch springform, Aluminum foil, Stand or hand mixer fitted with the paddle attachment, Large mixing bowl, Spatula or cake scraper, Parchment paper, Cake decorating piping tips and bags (optional).

PREPARATION:

MAKE THE CAKE:

Step 1: Preheat the oven to 350°F. Line the bottom of the 9-inch springform pan with parchment paper. Grease the paper and the sides of the pan with a cooking spray.

Step 2: In a food processor, add graham cookies and process into fine crumbs. Add melted butter and sugar. Process again until all is incorporated.

Step 3: Press the cookie mixture into a greased springform pan.

Step 4: Bake it for 10-15 minutes on 350°F. Set aside to cool. Reduce the oven's temperature to 325°F.

MAKE THE CHEESE:

Step 1: Add all cream cheese into a bowl of stand mixer (or use a large bowl and hand mixer with paddle attachment) equipped with the paddle attachment. Beat on low to medium until cream cheese softens and becomes smooth.

Step 2: Add sour cream, eggs, vanilla extract, Kahlua, sugar, and flour into the bowl with cream cheese. Beat the mixture with the paddle attachment until all is evenly incorporated and mixture becomes smooth. Do not overbeat, or the cake will crack.

Fold in chocolate chips. Mix with a spatula.

ASSEMBLE THE CAKE:

Step 1: Pour Kahlua cheese over the graham cookies crust.

Step 2: Prepare the water-bath. Cover the bottom of springform pan with aluminum foil. Place it into a larger ovenproof tray. Pour one inch of boiling water into the larger tray. (Do not let water get into the cheesecake).

BAKE THE CAKE:

Step 1: Bake the cake at 325°F for about one hour and ten minutes or until the center of the cake is set and not very wobbly. At 30-35 minutes into baking, cover the springform with aluminum foil to prevent burning of the top of the cake.

Step 2: After one hour and ten minutes turn the oven off and leave the cheesecake inside the oven (with oven door closed) for two hours.

Step 3: After two hours, set it aside to cool at room temperature. Cheesecake tastes best the next day. Once the cheesecake is cooled to a room temperature leave it overnight in the fridge.

MAKE THE FROSTING:

Step 1: Combine butter and powdered sugar in a bowl of stand mixer fitted with the paddle attachment (you can use a bowl and a hand mixer).

Beat on medium speed for 2 to 3 minutes until it is fully incorporated and becomes fluffy and light in color.

Step 2: Spoon by spoon, add farmers cheese and beat on medium speed for 2 to 3 minutes until it is fully incorporated and becomes light and fluffy.

Add vanilla extract and Kahlua. Beat for another 2-3 minutes.

If you decorate your cake, using cake decorating piping tips and bags, set aside and refrigerate 1/3 of the frosting for about an hour until it becomes firm.

This will be your cooled frosting. The rest of the frosting will be room temperature frosting. Cover top of cheesecake with frosting.

DECORATE THE CAKE:

If you are decorating your cake with piping tips, once you are ready to decorate your cake, remove the cooled frosting from the fridge.

Place the cooled frosting into a piping bag and start piping borders and flowers. You can also add food coloring. *(We recommend using natural food coloring instead of artificial colors).*

Kahlua Cheesecake will keep for up to five days in a fridge or one month in a freezer.

Oreo Cookies Cheesecake

INGREDIENTS:

FOR THE CAKE CRUST:

2 cups **Oreo Cookies**

1 ½ cups **Butter**, unsalted, softened

1/2 cup **Sugar,** cane, granulated

Cooking spray for greasing the springform pan

FOR THE CHEESE:

24 Oz **Cream Cheese**

3 **Eggs**

1 cup **Sugar,** cane, granulated

1 cup **Sour Cream**

1 cup **Oreo Cookies,** crushed

3 tablespoon **Flour,** all purpose

1/2 teaspoon **Vanilla**, extract, pure

FOR THE FROSTING:

6 Oz **Butter**, unsalted, softened

6 Oz **Farmer Cheese**

2 ½ cups **Sugar**, cane, powdered

1 teaspoon **Vanilla**, extract, pure

EQUIPMENT:

One 9-inch springform baking pan, One larger ovenproof tray or pan to fit 9-inch springform, Aluminum foil, Stand or hand mixer fitted with the paddle attachment, Zip lock bag and Rolling pin, Food processor, Large mixing bowl, Spatula, Cake scraper, Parchment paper, Cake decorating piping tips and bags (optional).

PREPARATION:

MAKE THE CAKE:

Step 1: Preheat the oven to 350°F. Line the bottom of the 9-inch springform pan with parchment paper. Grease the paper and the sides of the pan with a cooking spray.

Step 2: In a food processor, add Oreo cookies and process into fine crumbs. Add melted butter and sugar. Process again until all is incorporated.

Step 3: Press the cookie mixture into the greased springform pan.

Step 4: Bake it for 10-15 minutes on 350°F. Set aside to cool. Reduce the oven's temperature to 325°F.

MAKE THE CHEESE:

Step 1: Place Oreo cookies into a Ziplock bag. Crush cookies with a rolling pin into small (approximately 1/4 inches) crumbs. (Alternatively, you can pulse cookies in a food processor).

Step 2: Add all cream cheese into a bowl of stand mixer (or use a large bowl and hand mixer with paddle attachment) equipped with the paddle attachment. Beat on low to medium until cream cheese softens and becomes smooth.

Step 3: Add eggs (one at a time), sugar, sour cream, vanilla extract, and flour into the bowl with cream cheese. Beat the mixture with the paddle attachment until all is evenly incorporated and mixture becomes smooth. Do not overbeat, or the cake will crack.

Fold in crushed Oreo cookies. Mix with a spatula.

ASSEMBLE THE CAKE:

Step 1: Pour cheese batter over the Oreo cookies crust.

Step 2: Prepare the water-bath. Cover the bottom of springform pan with aluminum foil. Place it into a larger ovenproof tray. Pour one inch of boiling water into the larger tray. (Do not let water get into the cheesecake).

BAKE THE CAKE:

Step 1: Bake the cake at 325°F for about one hour and ten minutes or until the center of the cake is set and not very wobbly. At 30-35 minutes into baking, cover the springform with aluminum foil to prevent burning of the top of the cake.

Step 2: After one hour and ten minutes turn the oven off and leave the cheesecake inside the oven (with oven door closed) for two hours.

Step 3: After two hours, set it aside to cool at room temperature. Cheesecake tastes best the next day. Once the cheesecake is cooled to a room temperature leave it overnight in the fridge.

MAKE THE FROSTING:

Step 1: Combine butter and powdered sugar in a bowl of stand mixer fitted with the paddle attachment (you can use a bowl and a hand mixer).

Beat on medium speed for 2 to 3 minutes until it is fully incorporated and becomes fluffy and light in color.

Step 2: Spoon by spoon, add farmers cheese and beat on medium speed for 2 to 3 minutes until it is fully incorporated and becomes light and fluffy.

Add vanilla extract and beat for another 2-3 minutes.

If you decorate your cake, using cake decorating piping tips and bags, set aside and refrigerate 1/3 of the frosting for about an hour until it becomes firm.

This will be your cooled frosting. The rest of the frosting will be room temperature frosting.

Cover the top of cheesecake with frosting. Decorate with Oreo cookies.

DECORATE THE CAKE:

If you are decorating your cake with cake decorating tools, once you are ready to decorate your cake, remove the cooled frosting from the fridge.

Place the cooled frosting into a piping bag and start piping borders and flowers. You can also add food coloring. *(We recommend using natural food coloring instead of artificial colors).*

Oreo Cookies Cheesecake will keep for up to five days in a fridge or one month in a freezer.

Wild Blueberries Cheesecake

INGREDIENTS:

FOR THE CAKE:

1 ½ cups **Flour**, all-purpose

1/2 cup **Butter**, unsalted, melted

1/2 cup **Sugar,** granulated

1/2 cup **Sugar**, brown

1 **Egg**

2 tablespoons **Buttermilk** (or **Sour Cream**)

1 teaspoon **Baking Powder**

3/4 teaspoon **Baking Soda**

1/4 teaspoon **Salt,** sea, fine

2 teaspoons **Vanilla**, extract, pure

Cooking spray for greasing the springform pan

FOR THE SYRUP:

12 Oz **Blueberries**, wild, frozen

2 cups **Sugar,** cane, granulated

6 tablespoons **Water**

1 tablespoon **Cornstarch**, organic

1/2 tablespoon **Vanilla,** extract

FOR THE CHEESE:

24 Oz **Cream Cheese**

3 **Eggs**

1 cup **Sugar,** cane, granulated

3/4 cup **Sour Cream**

1 tablespoon **Flour,** all purpose

1 cup **Chocolate Chips**, white, bakers

FOR THE FROSTING:

6 Oz **Farmer cheese**

6 Oz **Butter**, unsalted, softened

2 ½ cups **Sugar**, cane, powdered

1/2 tablespoon **Vanilla,** pure, extract

FOR THE DECORATIONS:

1 cup **Chocolate**, white, shaved

8 Oz **Blueberries**, fresh

EQUIPMENT:

One 9-inch springform baking pan, One larger ovenproof tray or pan to fit 9-inch springform, Aluminum foil, Small saucepan, Stand or hand mixer fitted with the paddle attachment, Large mixing bowl, Spatula or cake scraper, Parchment paper, Cake decorating piping tips and bags (optional).

PREPARATION:

MAKE THE CAKE:

Step 1: With the cooking spray, grease the bottom and sides of 9-inch springform pan. Line the bottom with parchment paper (optional).

Step 2: In a large bowl, sift and combine flour, baking powder, baking soda, and salt.

Step 3: In a bowl of stand mixer fitted with the paddle attachment (you can use a bowl and a hand mixer) combine butter, sugar, brown sugar and eggs.

Mix on low speed until everything is well incorporated and achieves a smooth consistency.

Add vegetable oil, buttermilk and vanilla extract. Continue mixing until all is well incorporated.

Step 4: Separate flour mix onto 3 or 4 parts and add it in 3 or 4 batches, using a spatula to fold the mixture together until all is incorporated. Set aside.

MAKE THE SYRUP:

In a small saucepan combine blueberries, sugar, and water. Let the mixture boil over medium heat, constantly stirring it. Add cornstarch and vanilla.

Once the mixture thickens, turn off the heat and set the syrup aside to cool.

MAKE THE CHEESE:

Step 1: Add all cream cheese into a bowl of stand mixer (or use a large bowl and hand mixer with paddle attachment) equipped with the paddle attachment. Beat on low to medium until cream cheese softens and becomes smooth.

Step 2: Add eggs (one at a time), sugar, sour cream, vanilla extract, and flour. Beat the mixture with the paddle attachment until it becomes smooth. Do not overbeat or the cake will crack.

Step 3: Fold in white chocolate chips. Mix with a spatula.

Fold in blueberry syrup, gently mixing with a spatula. Do not over mix. Leave small chunks of the blueberries cluster together.

ASSEMBLE THE CAKE:

Step 1: Divide the cake batter onto eight parts. Pour first part of cake batter into the greased springform pan.

Step 2: Divide blueberry cheese onto eight parts. Pour first part of cream cheese next to the cake batter.

Repeat for all remaining cake and cream cheese batters. Alternate placing cake batter on top of cheese batter and vice versa.

Step 3: Prepare the water-bath. Cover the bottom of springform pan with aluminum foil.

Place it into a larger ovenproof tray. Pour one inch of boiling water into the larger tray. (Do not let water get into the cheesecake).

BAKE THE CAKE:

Step 1: Preheat the oven to 325F.

Bake the cake for about one hour and ten minutes, or until the center is set and not very wobbly. At 30-35 minutes into baking, cover the springform with aluminum foil to prevent burning of the top of the cake.

Step 2: After one hour and ten minutes turn the oven off and leave the cheesecake inside the oven (with oven door closed) for another two hours.

Step 3: After two hours, set it aside to cool at room temperature. Cheesecake tastes best the next day. Once the cheesecake is cooled to a room temperature leave it overnight in the fridge.

MAKE THE FROSTING:

Step 1: Combine butter and powdered sugar in a bowl of stand mixer fitted with the paddle attachment (you can use a bowl and a hand mixer).

Beat on medium speed for 2 to 3 minutes until it is fully incorporated and becomes fluffy and light in color.

Step 2: Spoon by spoon, add farmers cheese and beat on medium speed for 2 to 3 minutes until it is fully incorporated and becomes light and fluffy.

Add vanilla extract and beat for another 2-3 minutes.

If you decorate your cake using cake decorating piping tips and bags, set aside and refrigerate 1/3 of the frosting for about an hour until it becomes firm.

This will be your cooled frosting. The rest of the frosting will be room temperature frosting.

Step 3: Spread the room temperature frosting over your cake. Level the edges and surface of the cake with a spatula or scraper. Sprinkle the top of the cake with shredded coconut.

Use cooled frosting to decorate the cake using piping tips and bags.

DECORATE THE CAKE:

Cover the top of cheesecake with frosting. Place fresh blueberries on top.

If you are decorating your cake with cake decorating tools, once you are ready to decorate your cake, remove the cooled frosting from the fridge.

Place the cooled frosting into a piping bag and start piping borders and flowers. You can also add food coloring. *(We recommend using natural food coloring instead of artificial colors).*

Wild Blueberries Cheesecake will keep for up to five days in a fridge or one month in a freezer.

Red Velvet Cheesecake

INGREDIENTS:

FOR THE CAKE:

1 ½ cups **Flour**, all-purpose

1/2 cup **Butter**, unsalted, melted

1/2 cup **Sugar,** granulated

1/2 cup **Sugar**, brown

1/2 cup **Condensed milk**, sweetened

1/2 cup **Cocoa powder**, Dutch, processed, unsweetened

1 **Egg**

4 tablespoons **Beats**, raw, powder

2 tablespoons **Buttermilk**

1 teaspoon **Baking Powder**

3/4 teaspoon **Baking Soda**

1/4 teaspoon **Salt,** sea, pure

2 teaspoons **Vanilla**, extract, pure

Cooking spray for greasing the springform pan

FOR THE CHEESE:

16 Oz **Cream Cheese**

8 Oz **Farmer Cheese**

3 **Eggs**

1 cup **Sugar,** cane, granulated

1 cup **Heavy Cream**

1 tablespoon **Flour,** all purpose

1/2 teaspoon **Vanilla**, extract, pure

FOR THE FROSTING:

6 Oz **Butter**, unsalted, softened

6 Oz **Farmer Cheese**

4 cups **Sugar**, cane, powdered

1 teaspoon **Vanilla**, extract, pure

EQUIPMENT:

One 9-inch springform baking pan, 1 larger ovenproof tray or pan to fit 9-inch springform, aluminum foil; stand or hand mixer fitted with the paddle attachment, Large mixing bowl; Spatula or cake scraper, Parchment paper, Cake decorating piping tips and bags (optional).

PREPARATION:

MAKE THE CAKE:

Step 1: Line the bottom of the 9-inch springform pan with parchment paper. Grease the paper and the sides of the pan with a cooking spray.

Step 2: In a large bowl, sift and combine flour, baking powder, baking soda, and salt. Set the flour mixture aside.

Step 3: Combine butter, powdered beats, cocoa powder, sugar, brown sugar, and eggs.
in a bowl of stand mixer fitted with the paddle attachment (you can use a bowl and a hand mixer).

Mix on low speed until everything is incorporated and batter achieves a smooth consistency. Add vegetable oil, buttermilk, condensed milk, and vanilla extract. Continue mixing until all is incorporated.

Step 4: Separate flour mixture onto 3 or 4 parts and add it in 3 or 4 batches, using a spatula to fold the mixture together until all is incorporated. Set aside.

MAKE THE CHEESE:

Step 1: Add all cream cheese and farmers cheese into a bowl of stand mixer (or use a large bowl and hand mixer with paddle attachment) equipped with the paddle attachment. Beat on low to medium until cream cheese and farmers cheese soften and mixture becomes smooth.

Step 2: Add eggs (one at a time), sugar, heavy cream, vanilla extract and flour (little by little). Beat the mixture with the paddle attachment until all is evenly incorporated and mixture becomes smooth. Do not overbeat or the cake will crack.

ASSEMBLE THE CAKE:

Step 1: Pour one half of red velvet cake batter into the greased springform pan. Pour one half of cheese over the cake batter.

Pour second half of red velvet cake batter onto cheese. Pour second half of cheese batter over the cake batter.

Step 2: Prepare the water-bath. Cover the bottom of springform pan with aluminum foil. Place it into a larger ovenproof tray. Pour one inch of boiling water into the larger tray. (Do not let water get into the cheesecake).

BAKE THE CAKE:

Step 1: Preheat the oven to 325F. Bake the cake for about one hour and ten minutes, or until the center is set and not very wobbly. At 30-35 minutes into baking, cover the springform with aluminum foil to prevent burning of the top of the cake.

Step 2: After one hour and ten minutes turn the oven off and leave the cheesecake inside the oven (with oven door closed) for another two hours.

Step 3: After two hours, set it aside to cool at room temperature. Cheesecake tastes best the next day. Once the cheesecake is cooled to a room temperature leave it overnight in the fridge.

MAKE THE FROSTING:

Step 1: Combine butter and powdered sugar in a bowl of stand mixer fitted with the paddle attachment (you can use a bowl and a hand mixer).

Beat on medium speed for 2 to 3 minutes until it is fully incorporated and becomes fluffy and light in color.

Step 2: Spoon by spoon, add farmers cheese and beat on medium speed for 2 to 3 minutes until it is fully incorporated and becomes light and fluffy.

Add vanilla extract and beat for another 2-3 minutes.

If you decorate your cake, using cake decorating piping tips and bags, set aside and refrigerate 1/3 of the frosting for about an hour until it becomes firm.

This will be your cooled frosting. The rest of the frosting will be room temperature frosting.

Step 3: Spread the room temperature frosting over your cake. Level the edges and surface of the cake with a spatula or scraper.

Use cooled frosting to decorate the cake using piping tips and bags.

DECORATE THE CAKE:

If you are decorating your cake with cake decorating tools, once you are ready to decorate your cake, remove the cooled frosting from the fridge.

Place the cooled frosting into a piping bag and start piping borders and flowers. You can also add food coloring. *(We recommend using natural food coloring instead of artificial colors).*

Red Velvet Cheesecake will keep for up to five days in a fridge or one month in a freezer.

Nutella Cheesecake

INGREDIENTS:

FOR THE CAKE:

1 ½ cups **Flour**, all-purpose

1/2 cup **Butter**, unsalted, melted

1/2 cup **Sugar,** cane, granulated

1/2 cup **Sugar**, brown

1 **Egg**

1 cup **Chocolate chips**, dark, bakers

2 tablespoons **Buttermilk** (or **Sour cream**)

1 teaspoon **Baking Powder**

3/4 teaspoon **Baking Soda**

1/4 teaspoon **Salt,** sea, fine

2 teaspoons **Vanilla**, extract, pure

Cooking spray for greasing the springform pan

FOR THE CHEESE:

24 Oz **Cream Cheese**

3 **Eggs**

1 1/2 cups **Nutella**, Hazelnut spread

1 cup **Sour Cream**

1/2 cup **Sugar,** cane, granulated

1 tablespoon **Flour,** all purpose

1/2 teaspoon **Vanilla**, extract, pure

FOR THE GLAZE:

1 cup **Nutella**, Hazelnut spread

1 cup **Chocolate chips**, dark, bakers

1/2 cup **Heavy Cream**

1/2 teaspoon **Vanilla**, extract, pure

FOR THE FROSITING: *(Optional)*

6 Oz **Butter**, unsalted, softened

6 Oz **Farmer Cheese**

4 cups **Sugar**, cane, powdered

1 teaspoon **Vanilla**, extract, pure

EQUIPMENT:

One 9-inch springform baking pan, One larger ovenproof tray or pan to fit 9-inch springform, Aluminum foil, Stand or hand mixer fitted with the paddle attachment, Large mixing bowl, Spatula or cake scraper, Parchment paper, Cake decorating piping tips and bags (optional).

PREPARATION:

MAKE THE CAKE:

Step 1: Line the bottom of the 9-inch springform pan with parchment paper. Grease the paper and the sides of the pan with a cooking spray.

Step 2: In a large bowl, sift and combine flour, baking powder, baking soda, and salt. Set the flour mixture aside.

Step 3: Combine butter, sugar, brown sugar and eggs in a bowl of stand mixer fitted with the paddle attachment (you can use a bowl and a hand mixer).

Mix on low speed until everything is incorporated and batter achieves a smooth consistency. Add vegetable oil, buttermilk, and vanilla extract. Continue mixing until all is incorporated.

Step 4: Separate flour mixture onto 3 or 4 parts and add it in 3 or 4 batches, using a spatula to fold the mixture together until all is incorporated. Set aside.

Step 5: Fold in chocolate chips and mix with a spatula. Set aside.

MAKE THE CHEESE:

Step 1: Add all cream cheese into a bowl of stand mixer (or use a large bowl and hand mixer with paddle attachment) equipped with the paddle attachment. Beat on low to medium until cream cheese softens and becomes smooth.

Step 2: Add eggs (one at a time), sugar, buttermilk, vanilla extract and flour (little by little). Beat the mixture with the paddle attachment until it becomes smooth. Do not overbeat or the cake will crack.

Add Nutella and beat again for 2-3 minutes. Do not overbeat or the cake will crack.

ASSEMBLE THE CAKE:

Step 1: Pour cake batter into the greased springform pan. Pour cheese batter over the cake batter.

Step 2: Prepare the water-bath. Cover the bottom of springform pan with aluminum foil. Place it into a larger ovenproof tray. Pour one inch of boiling water into the larger tray. (Do not let water get into the cheesecake).

BAKE THE CAKE:

Step 1: Preheat the oven to 325F. Bake the cake for about one hour and ten minutes, or until the center is set and not very wobbly. At 30-35 minutes into baking, cover the springform with aluminum foil to prevent burning of the top of the cake.

Step 2: After one hour and ten minutes turn the oven off and leave the cheesecake inside the oven (with oven door closed) for another two hours.

Step 3: After two hours, set it aside to cool at room temperature. Cheesecake tastes best the next day. Once the cheesecake is cooled to a room temperature leave it overnight in the fridge.

MAKE THE GLAZE:

Over a water bath, combine Nutella, chocolate chips, heavy cream, and vanilla extract. Mix with a whisk until Nutella and chocolate chips melt and all is evenly incorporated. Set aside to cool.

MAKE THE FROSTING: *(Optional)*

Step 1: Combine butter and powdered sugar in a bowl of stand mixer fitted with the paddle attachment (you can use a bowl and a hand mixer).

Beat on medium speed for 2 to 3 minutes until it is fully incorporated and becomes fluffy and light in color.

Step 2: Spoon by spoon, add farmers cheese and beat on medium speed for 2 to 3 minutes until it is fully incorporated and becomes light and fluffy.

Add vanilla extract and beat for another 2-3 minutes.

If you decorate your cake, using cake decorating piping tips and bags, set aside and refrigerate 1/3 of the frosting for about an hour until it becomes firm.

This will be your cooled frosting. The rest of the frosting will be room temperature frosting.

Step 3: Spread the room temperature frosting over your cake. Level the edges and surface of the cake with a spatula or scraper. Sprinkle the top of the cake with shredded coconut.

Use cooled frosting to decorate the cake using piping tips and bags.

DECORATE THE CAKE:

Cover top of cheesecake with warm Nutella chocolate glaze.

If you are decorating your cake with cake decorating tools, once you are ready to decorate your cake, remove the cooled frosting from the fridge.

Place the cooled frosting into a piping bag and start piping borders and flowers. You can also add food coloring. *(We recommend using natural food coloring instead of artificial colors).*

Nutella Cheesecake will keep for up to five days in a fridge or one month in a freezer.

Snickers Peanut Butter Cheesecake

INGREDIENTS:

FOR THE CAKE:

1 ½ cups **Flour**, all-purpose

1/2 cup **Butter**, unsalted, melted

1/2 cup **Sugar**, cane, granulated

1/2 cup **Sugar**, brown

1 **Egg**

1 cup **Cocoa powder**, Dutch, unsweetened

1 cup **Chocolate chips**, mini, dark, bakers

2 tablespoons **Buttermilk** (or **Sour cream**)

1 teaspoon **Baking Powder**

3/4 teaspoon **Baking Soda**

1/4 teaspoon **Salt**, sea, fine

2 teaspoons **Vanilla**, extract, pure

Cooking spray for greasing the springform pan

FOR THE CHEESE:

24 Oz **Cream Cheese**

3 **Eggs**

1 ½ cups **Peanut butter**, smooth

1 cup **Snickers**, mini, chopped

1/2 cup **Sugar,** cane, granulated

1 cup **Sour Cream**

1 tablespoon **Flour,** all purpose

1/2 teaspoon **Vanilla**, extract, pure

FOR THE GLAZE:

1 ½ cups **Chocolate chips**, dark, bakers

1/2 cup **Heavy Cream**

1/2 teaspoon **Vanilla**, extract, pure

FOR THE FROSTING: *(Optional)*

6 Oz **Butter**, unsalted, softened

6 Oz **Farmer Cheese**

4 cups **Sugar**, cane, powdered

1 teaspoon **Vanilla**, extract, pure

EQUIPMENT:

One 9-inch springform baking pan, One larger ovenproof tray or pan to fit 9-inch springform, Aluminum foil, Stand or hand mixer fitted with the paddle attachment, Large mixing bowl, Spatula or cake scraper, Kitchen knife, Parchment paper, Cake decorating piping tips and bags (optional).

PREPARATION:

MAKE THE CAKE:

Step 1: Line the bottom of the 9-inch springform pan with parchment paper. Grease the paper and the sides of the pan with a cooking spray.

Step 2: In a large bowl, sift and combine flour, baking powder, baking soda, and salt. Set the flour mixture aside.

Step 3: Combine butter, sugar, brown sugar and eggs in a bowl of stand mixer fitted with the paddle attachment (you can use a bowl and a hand mixer).

Mix on low speed until everything is incorporated and batter achieves a smooth consistency. Add vegetable oil, buttermilk, and vanilla extract. Continue mixing until all is incorporated.

Step 4: Separate flour mixture onto 3 or 4 parts and add it in 3 or 4 batches, using a spatula to fold the mixture together until all is incorporated. Set aside.

Step 5: Fold in chocolate chips and incorporate them with a spatula. Set aside.

MAKE THE CHEESE:

Step 1: Cut mini Snickers bars onto eight pieces each. Set aside.

Step 2: Add all cream cheese into a bowl of stand mixer (or use a large bowl and hand mixer with paddle attachment) equipped with the paddle attachment. Beat on low to medium until cream cheese softens and becomes smooth.

Step 3: Add eggs (one at a time), sugar, sour cream, vanilla extract and flour (little by little). Beat the mixture with the paddle attachment until it becomes smooth.

Add peanut butter and beat again for 3-4 minutes. Do not overbeat or the cake will crack.

Step 4: Fold in pieces of Snickers bars. Mix with a spatula to incorporate.

ASSEMBLE THE CAKE:

Step 1: Pour cake batter into greased the springform pan. Pour peanut butter cheese over the cake batter.

Step 2: Prepare the water-bath. Cover the bottom of springform pan with aluminum foil. Place it into a larger ovenproof tray. Pour one inch of boiling water into the larger tray. (Do not let water get into the cheesecake).

BAKE THE CAKE:

Step 1: Preheat the oven to 325°F.

Bake the cake for about one hour and ten minutes, or until the center is set and not very wobbly. At 30-35 minutes into baking, cover the springform with aluminum foil to prevent burning of the top of the cake.

Step 2: After one hour and ten minutes turn the oven off and leave the cheesecake inside the oven (with oven door closed) for another two hours.

Step 3: After two hours, set it aside to cool at room temperature. Cheesecake tastes best the next day. Once the cheesecake is cooled to a room temperature leave it overnight in the fridge.

MAKE THE GLAZE:

Over a water bath, combine chocolate chips, heavy cream, and vanilla extract. Mix with a whisk until chocolate chips melt and all is evenly incorporated. Set aside to cool.

MAKE THE FROSTING: *(Optional)*

Step 1: Combine butter and powdered sugar in a bowl of stand mixer fitted with the paddle attachment (you can use a bowl and a hand mixer).

Beat on medium speed for 2 to 3 minutes until it is fully incorporated and becomes fluffy and light in color.

Step 2: Spoon by spoon, add farmers cheese and beat on medium speed for 2 to 3 minutes until it is fully incorporated and becomes light and fluffy.

Add vanilla extract and beat for another 2-3 minutes.

If you decorate your cake, using cake decorating piping tips and bags, set aside and refrigerate 1/3 of the frosting for about an hour until it becomes firm.

This will be your cooled frosting. The rest of the frosting will be room temperature frosting.

Step 3: Spread the room temperature frosting over your cake. Level the edges and surface of the cake with a spatula or scraper. Sprinkle the top of the cake with shredded coconut.

Use cooled frosting to decorate the cake using piping tips and bags.

DECORATE THE CAKE:

Cover top of cheesecake with warm chocolate glaze.

If you are decorating your cake with cake decorating tools, once you are ready to decorate your cake, remove the cooled frosting from the fridge.

Place the cooled frosting into a piping bag and start piping borders and flowers. You can also add food coloring. *(We recommend using natural food coloring instead of artificial colors).*

Snickers Peanut Butter Cheesecake will keep for up to five days in a fridge or one month in a freezer.

Tropical Paradise Cheesecake

INGREDIENTS:

FOR THE CAKE:

2 cups **Graham cookies,** Honey Maid brand

1 ½ cups **Butter**, unsalted, softened

1/2 cup **Sugar,** cane, granulated

Cooking spray for greasing the springform pan

FOR THE CHEESE:

32 Oz **Cream Cheese**

4 **Eggs**

1 cup **Sugar,** cane, granulated

1 cup **Sour Cream**

3/4 cup **Coconut,** shredded, unsweetened

1/2 cup **Apricots,** dried

1/2 cup **Walnuts,** chopped

3 tablespoon **Flour,** all purpose

1/2 teaspoon **Vanilla**, extract, pure

FOR THE FROSTING:

6 Oz **Butter**, unsalted, softened

6 Oz **Farmer Cheese**

2 ½ cups **Sugar**, cane, powdered

1 teaspoon **Vanilla**, extract, pure

EQUIPMENT:

One 9-inch springform baking pan, One larger ovenproof tray or pan to fit 9-inch springform, Aluminum foil, Stand or hand mixer fitted with the paddle attachment, Large mixing bowl, Spatula or cake scraper, Parchment paper, Cake decorating piping tips and bags (optional).

PREPARATION:

MAKE THE CAKE:

Step 1: Preheat the oven to 350°F. Line the bottom of the 9-inch springform pan with parchment paper. Grease the paper and the sides of the pan with a cooking spray.

Step 2: In a food processor, add graham cookies and process into fine crumbs. Add melted butter and sugar. Process again until all is incorporated.

Step 3: Press the cookie mixture into a greased springform pan.

Step 4: Bake it for 10-15 minutes on 350°F. Set aside to cool. Reduce the oven's temperature to 325°F.

MAKE THE CHEESE:

Step 1: Add all cream cheese into a bowl of stand mixer (or use a large bowl and hand mixer with paddle attachment) equipped with the paddle attachment. Beat on low to medium until cream cheese softens and becomes smooth.

Step 2: Add eggs (one at a time), sugar, sour cream, vanilla extract, and flour into the bowl with cheese. Beat the mixture with the paddle attachment until all is evenly incorporated and mixture becomes smooth. Do not overbeat, or the cake will crack.

Step 3: Cut dried apricots onto small (1/4 inch) pieces. Fold in shredded coconut, apricots, and nuts. Mix with a spatula until all is evenly incorporated.

ASSEMBLE THE CAKE:

Step 1: Pour cheese over the graham cookies crust.

Step 2: Prepare the water-bath. Cover the bottom of springform pan with aluminum foil. Place it into a larger ovenproof tray. Pour one inch of boiling water into the larger tray. (Do not let water get into the cheesecake).

BAKE THE CAKE:

Step 1: Bake the cake at 325°F for about one hour and ten minutes or until the center of the cake is set and not very wobbly. At 30-35 minutes into baking, cover the springform with aluminum foil to prevent burning of the top of the cake.

Step 2: After one hour and ten minutes turn the oven off and leave the cheesecake inside the oven (with oven door closed) for two hours.

Step 3: After two hours, set it aside to cool at room temperature. Cheesecake tastes best the next day. Once the cheesecake is cooled to a room temperature leave it overnight in the fridge.

MAKE THE FROSTING:

Step 1: Combine butter and powdered sugar in a bowl of stand mixer fitted with the paddle attachment (you can use a bowl and a hand mixer).

Beat on medium speed for 2 to 3 minutes until it is fully incorporated and becomes fluffy and light in color.

Step 2: Spoon by spoon, add farmers cheese and beat on medium speed for 2 to 3 minutes until it is fully incorporated and becomes light and fluffy.

Add vanilla extract and beat for another 2-3 minutes.

If you decorate your cake, using cake decorating piping tips and bags, set aside and refrigerate 1/3 of the frosting for about an hour until it becomes firm.

This will be your cooled frosting. The rest of the frosting will be room temperature frosting. Cover top of cheesecake with frosting.

DECORATE THE CAKE:

Cover the top of cheesecake with frosting. Sprinkle with shredded coconut.

If you are decorating your cake with cake decorating tools, once you are ready to decorate your cake, remove the cooled frosting from the fridge.

Place the cooled frosting into a piping bag and start piping borders and flowers. You can also add food coloring. *(We recommend using natural food coloring instead of artificial colors).*

Tropical Paradise Cheesecake will keep for up to five days in a fridge or one month in a freezer.

Thank You for Purchasing This Book!

I create and test recipes for you. I hope you enjoyed these recipes.

Your review of this book helps me succeed & grow. If you enjoyed this book, please leave me a short (1-2 sentence) review on Amazon.

Thank you so much for reviewing this book!

Do you have any questions?
Email me at: **Maria@BRILLIANTkithenideas.com**

MARIA SOBININA
BRILLIANT kitchen ideas

Would you like to learn Cake Decorating techniques and tips?

We have series of educational videos on baking and cake decorating.

www. BRILLIANTkitchenideas.com

Printed in Great Britain
by Amazon